Rilke on Love

Warbler Press

Biographical note © 2020 Warbler Press
A Note on the Edition and About This Book © 2020 by Ulrich Baer
Translation © 2020 by Ulrich Baer

ISBN 978-1-7345881-2-5 (paperback)
ISBN 978-1-7345881-3-2 (e-book)

warblerpress.com

Printed in the United States of America. This edition is printed
with chlorine-free ink on acid-free interior paper made from 30%
post-consumer waste recycled material.

Current and forthcoming titles in the
Warbler Press Contemplations series at
warblerpress.com

Rilke on Love

Rainer Maria Rilke

EDITED AND TRANSLATED BY ULRICH BAER

A Note on the Text

There exists no comprehensive edition of all of Rainer Maria Rilke's correspondence. This is surprising, given Rilke's status as one of the great poets of world literature. The absence of an authoritative source occasionally turns the practice of reading Rilke's letters into a treasure hunt rather than a well-charted journey into the poet's heart and mind. Rilke's correspondence with his many interlocutors, ranging from illustrious authors, publishers, and patrons, to youthful admirers, lovers, and family members—all of whom received Rilke's full attention in even the shortest missive—has appeared in an assortment of books, including private printings found only in a few of the world's libraries and archives. A good number of editions have been released in Germany, some with extensive notes and others that provide sparse additional information. This collection is drawn from different editions of Rilke's letters published originally in Germany and France, in addition to passages found in archives in Europe and the United States. All translations are original.

Contents

RILKE ON LOVE

When love begins 1

When love grows...33

When love ends...61

When love endures...91

About This Book...*118*

Rainer Maria Rilke...*120*

Rilke on Love

When love begins...

BUT now, when weeks of spring are finally here,

Something slowly broke me from

The unconscious, darkest year.

Something placed my poor and pulsing life

Into another's open hand

Who does not know, what I was still the day
before.

Love Song

How shall I hold my soul, so

that it does not lean on yours? How should I

lift it over you to other things?

I so would like to stow

it near something lost in darkness

in a strange and quiet spot, so

it does not quiver on when your depths quiver.

But everything that touches us, touches me and
you,

draws us together like a musician's bow,

which yields *one* voice from two taut strings.

On which instrument have we been strung?

Which player holds us in his hand?

Oh, sweetest song.

I HAVE experienced, over and over again, that there is hardly anything more difficult than to love one another. It is work, day labor, truly a daily chore: God knows, there is no other word for it. You see, young people are not being prepared for such difficult loving; for convention has tried to turn this most complicated and extreme relation into something easy and effortless, and created the illusion that anyone is capable of love. This is not the case. To love is difficult, and it is more difficult than other tasks because in other conflicts, nature itself urges us to pull ourselves together and gather ourselves with all our strength. But once love grows more intense, there also grows the attraction to surrender ourselves entirely. But really, can this amount to anything beautiful: to give oneself to the other not as a whole and coherent self but by coincidence, piece by piece, just as it happens to come about? Can such a giving away of oneself, which so closely resembles a throwing away and tearing apart, amount to anything good, can it be happiness, joy, progress? No, it cannot...When you give someone flowers, you arrange them beforehand, don't you? But young people in love throw themselves at one another with the impatience and haste of their passion, and they do not even notice what lack of mutual respect characterizes this disorderly surrender. They notice it only with amazement and displeasure by way of the rift that arises from all of this disorder between them. And once discord exists between them, the confusion grows with each passing day; neither of them has anything that is not shattered but pure and unspoiled around them, and amidst all of the bleakness of a break-up they seek to hold on to the illusion of their happiness (for all of this was supposed to be in the name of happiness). Alas, they hardly manage to recall what they had meant by happiness. In their uncertainty, each of them grows increasingly unjust toward the other; while intending to please each other, they now touch each other only impatiently and in a dominating manner. And in the effort to escape somehow from the intolerable and unbearable condition of their confusion, they commit the greatest mistake that can be made in a relationship between humans: they become impatient. They push themselves to reach closure by arriving at a final decision, as they believe; they try to define once and for all their relationship, whose unexpected changes frightened them, so that from now on it can remain the same *"forever"* (as they say). This is only the final mistake in this long chain of interlocking errors. Even what is dead cannot be held on to absolutely (for it disintegrates and changes in its nature); how much less may something living and alive be treated definitively once and for all. Life is in its essence transformation, and human relations, which are an extract of life, are the most mutable things of all; they rise and fall from minute to minute, and people in love are those individuals in whose relation and touch no moment is like any other. They are people between whom nothing habitual, which had already once occurred, ever takes place, but only countless new, unexpected, unheard-of things. There are relationships that must be a vast and almost unbearable happiness, but they can take place only between people blessed with abundance and between those where each individual is rich, focused, and mindful. Only two expansive, deep, individual worlds can unite them.—Young people—this is obvious—cannot attain such a relationship, but, if they understand their life correctly, they can gradually mature into such happiness and prepare for it. When they love, they must not forget that they are beginners, bunglers of life, apprentices in love—they must *learn* love, and that requires (as for *all* learning) quiet, patience, and concentration!

THE MORE one is, the richer is everything one experiences. If you want to have a deep love in your life, you must save up for it and collect and gather honey.

THE PRIVILEGE to cause joy is given to us far less frequently than one would think, partly owing to our often rigid incapacity to receive and partly owing to the imprecision and vagueness between people (this may always have been an obstacle), which has increased even more in confusing times. After all, even the most appropriate gift still requires the receiver to accommodate himself to an extreme degree. In cases of "well-matched" giving, in contrast, even this effort belongs to the natural movement of the person who receives the gift.

JUST as you press a cloth to stifle bated breath,

no: just as you press it firm against a wound,

from which life rushes, in one blast,

to escape, I held you tight: I saw

you turned bright-red because of me. Who will express,

what happened to us here? We made up all the things,

for which we'd had no time. I strangely grew

with each excited leap beyond my youth,

and you, beloved, spread some kind of wildest

childhood over my heart.

[to Lou Andreas-Salomé]

SEXUALITY is difficult, indeed. But we have been burdened with difficult tasks, almost everything serious is difficult, and everything is serious. If only you recognize that and succeed, based on *your* gifts and way of being, on *your* experiences, childhood and strength (and not based on conventions and customs), to forge your very own relationship to your sexuality, then you no longer need to be afraid of losing yourself and becoming unworthy of your greatest gift.

Bodily lust is a sensual experience no different from pure seeing or the pure sensation with which a delicious fruit fills our tongue. It is a tremendous and limitless experience that is given to us as knowledge of the whole world, as knowledge in all of its fullness and glory. The fact that we experience it is not bad in itself. What is bad is that almost everyone abuses and wastes this experience by turning it into a stimulant for those moments when life gets dull, and as a distraction rather than an opportunity to gather oneself into a higher state. Humans have done the same with food: by thinking of food in terms of either lack or excess, they have obscured the clarity of this need. All of the deep and simple needs through which life renews itself have become muddled in this way. But each individual has the power to clarify these for himself and to live clearly (even if not everyone, then at least someone who is alone and does not overly depend on others). It is up to him to remember that all beauty, whether that of animals or plants, is a quiet, enduring form of love and longing. He can look at the animal and truly see it, just as he sees a plant, uniting, multiplying, and growing patiently and willingly not to obey the dictates of physical lust or physical pain but to obey laws that are greater than lust and pain and more powerful than will and resistance. If man only received this secret more humbly of which the earth abounds even in the tiniest things, if man only bore this secret more seriously! If man only accepted this burden and sensed how terribly difficult it is, instead of taking it lightly! If man only were properly reverent and awed by his fertility, which is one and the same, whether of the spirit or the flesh. For mental creativity also originates in the flesh. In its essence it is the same, and nothing but a quieter, more ecstatic and more everlasting repetition of physical lust. "The notion of being a creator and of procreating and creating things," is nothing without its unending great confirmation and actualization in the world, it is nothing until it has been affirmed a thousand times over by the things and animals around us. The pleasure we take in our power to create is so indescribably beautiful and rich only because it is full of inherited memories of the procreation and birthing of millions of beings. A single creative thought brings back to life a thousand forgotten nights of love, which endow this thought with splendor and importance. Those who come together at night and are entwined in the rhythms of physical lust carry out an important task. They gather sweetness, depth and strength for the song of some future poet who will rise to give voice to unspeakable pleasure. They conjure the future. Even when they are wrong and blindly embrace one another, this future arrives nonetheless. It arrives in the form of a new human being, and out of this apparently arbitrary and accidental event, the law asserts itself that causes a resilient strong sperm to push toward the egg cell advancing openly toward it. Do not be distracted by surfaces; in the depths everything becomes law. Those who live this secret falsely and badly (and there are many) lose it only for themselves and still unwittingly pass it on like an unopened letter. Don't get confused by the multitude of names and the complicated nature of all of these cases. Perhaps everything falls under a great collective longing for maternity. The beauty of the virgin as a being "that (as you so nicely put it) hasn't yet accomplished anything," is the first tender stirring, preparation and fearful longing of maternity. The beauty of a mother is maternity that has found its calling, and in a woman of old age lives her tremendous remembrance. Even in man there is maternity, it seems to me, both physical and mental. His act of procreation is also a kind of birthing, and it is like giving birth when he creates from inner abundance. Perhaps the two genders are more closely related than we think. The great renewal of the world may indeed happen when man and woman, freed from all misguided sentiments and false desires, will no longer seek out one another as opposites but come together as brother and sister, as neighbors, and ultimately as human beings. It will happen when men and women join together to seriously and patiently bear the heavy burden of the flesh that has been placed upon them. But for all of this, which may be possible for many people in the future, a solitary individual can lay a strong foundation with his own, steadier hands. This, dear Sir, is the reason why you should love your solitude and endure, and even celebrate the pain it causes you. You tell me that those close to you are far away: this means that around you space is beginning to open up. If everything that is close to you seems far away, then space already extends for you into a great distance, all the way to the stars. You should rejoice in this expansion of yourself; nobody can follow you there. But be kind to those you leave behind by being steady and calm in your dealings with them. Do not torment them with your doubts and do not frighten them with your confidence or joy, which they cannot understand. Find something basic and reliable that you have in common with them, and which does not necessarily have to change while you go through your transformations. Love them for the way they live life in a different form. Go easy on those who are afraid of the loneliness in which you have confidence, due to their advancing age. Avoid adding to the drama that always takes place between parents and children. It consumes a lot of the children's strength and uses up the adults' love, which offers support and nourishment even when this love fails to understand. Don't ask others for advice and don't expect to be understood. Instead, believe in a love that is being safeguarded for you like an inheritance. Have faith that this love will be with you as a force and a blessing while you go very, very far!

To BE spontaneously free in one's body, what greatest pleasure!

ONCE in love, once ablaze, one must no longer consider oneself unhappy; whoever had gained access
one time to the blessedness of love *is in it,* and for him
all deprivation and longing are henceforth only the
weight and gravity of his plenitude! It is possible that
love will then become pain, suffering and despair for
him, and that he can no longer apply this fullness *there*
where it had originally been desired and anticipated.
But isn't every young man always in the position of
a "sorcerer's apprentice" whose enraptured heart
unleashes powerful storms he cannot master, and
from which he rescues himself (perhaps *has* to rescue
himself) to maintain that other, logical, productive
and apparently sober measure of his life, which contradicts love and only occasionally allows our senses
to have an experience as a kind of balancing act for
the exaggerated tensions pulling in other directions.

PHYSIOLOGICAL research discovers ever more astonishing circumstances with regard to the distribution of masculine and feminine elements within all beings; we are so far from thinking that there is an unequivocal here and there. In this domain, everything is most finely and secretly calibrated, and it can very easily happen, and not only "abnormally," that the kind of complementary affinity happens between two young women that justifies for them even the most intimate sensuality. I suspect that such raptures are filled with much more innocence than many "normal" relations and, that once it will be possible to acknowledge how entirely natural and guileless such delights are, it might also be possible to strangely unburden the confused, overwrought efforts at love between woman and man. For this love surely faces as its most insurmountable and disastrous difficulty the tremendous emphasis of its one "goal," as if all the paths and dead ends of our emotions could be so sweetly completed. But this transforms love from something secret into something conspicuous, and this alone distorts it immensely. People in love, since they see no end to giving and receiving and in whose hands everything becomes nameless, should actually not even know *even before each other* (this is how I always imagine it) whether among the countless instances of bliss in their union there might also have been one which (rightly or wrongly, perhaps both) is considered the most extreme.

Now you may already have guessed a little *what* I expect of this genuine intercourse of love within one gender: that it prepares in the individuals who undergo it (maybe quite temporarily) a different way of evaluation things where it is not the one goal—which can never be reached fully *there*—does not entirely dominate, although it could be there, according to its intensity. Instead, within this from the outset more intimate exchange, many things would be set free and used up (especially concerning the man) that otherwise overwhelm and bury the other gender without, strictly speaking, meaning it. I want to think of such periods of love as a veritable school for love that covers the most sensuous touches and embraces as well as the tenderly shared hovering of the spirit, where the little temple is placed alternately among youthful male lovers and then among females, as if their more fraught attractions later in life depended a tiny bit upon the tender experiences and exercises that occur easily and pre-seriously among themselves.

In this area everything is in such disarray for us that one should not shrink from even the most daring suggestion, as long as it might chart a path toward change in this legally protected rubble. And how do we finally determine whether something is "daring"—it is morality, which has long been recognized to create great confusion especially when it intervenes in the realm of love and falsifies the degree of appearances that are incommensurate when taken out of context. If we ever have a sense of being blocked by morality, we finally ought to become suspicious only about the blockage but not about our impulses. The sense of a totality, the always renewed feeling of the unity of our own life and those indescribable moments during which death no longer prompts our suspicion: these are the building blocks for everybody's private court of law where his responsibility will be judged.

For such relationships, it remains definitive what applies to all transformations between two human beings: one must *never* view and assess a relationship in all of its details from the *outside:* what two people could give and grant each other in their mutual confidence remains forever a secret of their always indescribable intimacy. If they thought at a particular moment that they could create even more tender pleasures for each other, this might have been a small error since they did not serve their happiness but their longing in this way, and thus stirred up their blood in ways that could prove distressing after the fact—perhaps, but who is to judge that? Perhaps they were justified after all in thus surrendering, which is so indescribably innocent, like everything in love that is born of a simple having-to-do and not-knowing-any-differently—nobody may dare to judge what happened there from the outside. Such rapture and such joy, no matter how far they go, may yield a moment of transformation that concerns nothing but *the soul.* And since this had seemed like a new kind of experience reached through what is called sensuality, one may have been all along in a truly advanced state ahead of one's soul, which had been transported there through rapture. All of this is so much more secretly connected that we must face these forces with humility. Our innocence will provide the way to resist them, because it is indestructible within us as long as we do not let ourselves be convinced of our guilt. The uncertainties and insecurities in these areas have increased so terribly in our time that a young person can almost never count on having the kind of adviser and protector whom he would need, not even in the figure of his mother (who is helpless like the whole world). For this reason alone, one ought to rely unerringly and guilelessly on one's innocence to get one's bearings. Sensible people have long struggled to free love relations within one's own gender of the ugly suspicions heaped there by convention—but even this effort and viewpoint does not seem the right one. It isolates a process that ought to be considered always only within the full range of its contexts, and it turns an inexpressibly unique occurrence into something general and even ordinary only because it could engulf anyone. And ultimately this approach retains only the physical manifestation of such an event and forgets in what inaccessible and exuberant relations this one thing (which cannot really be described) is embedded. We do not know *where* to locate the center of a love relation and what would constitute its most extreme, unsurpassable, and most ecstatic dimension: sometimes this center may be found in the final and sweetest physical intimacy (also between women) but *nobody* ought to be the judge of that, except the discreet responsibility of these lovers themselves in their enjoyment. This mutual giving themselves to each other would not mean that they have gone astray; at most, they could veer off their path by the insecurity whether they in fact afforded each other this lasting intensification that is the ultimate pleasure and longing of love. Only if this created something between them that would cause them to become more difficult, murkier, and more opaque to each other, would they be wrong to surrender to these experiences. *Then,* however, there would be the danger that they remain stuck in them. For *no* tenderness of love must have power over love itself, and no tenderness must impose itself with the force of mindless repetition, but an entirely new

tenderness must be born always anew out of the inex-
haustibility of our emotions.

IF I did not resist the lover, this happened because of all the ways in which one human being can take possession of another, her unstoppable approach alone seemed to me the right one. In my exposed state, I also did not want to *avoid* her; but I longed to pass through her! So that she would be a window for me into the expanded universe of existence...not a mirror.

THERE are no established rules of conduct for those who have *not* married each other. But that makes it possible to establish a kind of relation there for which no guidelines are envisioned, and which would be a union beyond all conventions.

IT IS possible to love so *extensively* that the short-comings of the object of one's love become touching, even wonderful, and an incentive to be all the more loving!

I HAVE never understood how a genuine, elementary, thoroughly true love can be unrequited since it is nothing but the urgent and blessed appeal for another person to be beautiful, abundant, great, heartfelt, unforgettable: nothing but the surging commitment for him to become something.—And who could refuse this appeal when it is directed at him, elects him from among millions, chooses him, he who might have lived obscured by his fate or unattainable in the midst of fame...for such a love cannot be seized, taken, or contained by anyone: it is so absolutely intended to be passed on beyond the individual, and requires the beloved only to provide the ultimate momentum for its future orbiting among the stars.

Eros

Masks! Masks! We should blind Eros now.

Who tolerates his beaming face,

when like the summer solstice

he interrupts springtime foreplay.

How, unexpectedly, while simply chatting

things change and become serious... Something
screamed...

And he casts the nameless veil

like the inside of a temple over them.

Ah, lost, suddenly, so lost!

Divine beings are quick to embrace.

Life twisted, fate was born.

And inside a source wells up and weeps.

WHEN would a man have found time to explore the life of a young woman he loves? He believes to know her at the first fleeting encounter, and later forgets it; for it is still too new for men to love another human being, an entire human being who has her own, uncertain, growing life.

If one could only look back at every human countenance that had even just once seriously and openly turned toward us, without any self-reproach for having betrayed or overlooked it. But one lives in the density of one's own body, which imposes its particular measure already in purely physical terms (because after all there is nothing to go on but this physical I), and since one lives, I think, in the awkwardness of this body and confined and imprisoned by the surrounding world in which one moves...one is not always as free, as loving, and as innocent as one should be able to be according to one's proper resources and convictions. And frequently insecurity and distractedness limit us further. What big-hearted confidence in oneself would be necessary to respond to every voice that reaches us with the truest sense of hearing and the most undistracted reply.

WHY, by God, do we spend our lives in conventions that restrict us like a tight costume and prevent us from realizing the invisible soul, this dancer underneath the stars!

OUR emotions cannot do anything but become greater through empathy. From empathy to imitation it is yet a different path—in a sense a backtracking. Empathy is directed toward the inside, whereas imitation leads back outside into visibility. As such, it is actually the immediate loss of that which can be claimed through the emotion of empathy. But in the direction toward the inside followed by empathy, of this I am sure, one cannot go too far. The further one ventures there, the more dependably one will tap into a previously unknown vein of one's own feelings. I consider imitators mostly to be individuals who did not muster enough empathy and who instead turned around halfway and, by backtracking their footprints, reached the outside again. Any engagement with a work of art would be absolutely hopeless without an empathic response that would almost lead to one's own annihilation, but ultimately returns us to ourselves richer, stronger, and more capable of feeling. Empathy is humility, imitation is vanity—and thus it ought to be possible soon to notice whether one intends one or the other.

WHAT ruthless magnificence and yet how *terrible* to ignite love, what conflagration, what disaster, what doom. To be on fire *yourself,* of course, if one is capable of it: that may well be worth one's life and one's death.

WHAT meadows are as fragrant as your hands?

Do you feel how outside fragrance stands

grounded strong in your resistance?

The stars compose an image high above

Give me your mouth to soften, love,

Ah, all of your hair remains untouched.

See, I want to surround you with yourself

and let wilting desire rise again

from along your eyebrow's edge;

Like adding insides to your eyelids

with my caresses I will blot

from view what you now see from any spot.

When love grows…

The Lovers

See how they grow more toward each other
All turns into spirit in their pulsating veins
Their bodies tremble like axes
Around which circles a heat-filled strain.
Thirsting, they find something to drink.
Rise and behold: they find something to see.
Let them sink deeply into each other
To endure, outlast, and for each other—be.

To BE close to another person who holds *opposing* views while being a deep, committed friend can be a wonderful, shaping influence. For as long as one is forced to consider (as one is frequently vis-à-vis parents and older people in general) anything different in every instance to be false, bad, hostile instead of purely and simply—different, one will not enter into an unforced and just relation with the world where all things, part and counterpart, are meant to have a place, including myself and the person most different from me. And only when such a complete world is presupposed and accepted, will one succeed in arranging one's own interiority with its internal contrasts and contradictions expansively, broadly and with air to breathe.

LOVE—most sacred earnestness and yet most beautiful of games.

DON'T let yourself be distracted in your solitude by the fact that something inside of you wishes to escape from it. In fact, if you deploy this wish calmly and deliberately you can use it like an instrument to expand your solitude across new and rich regions. People have solved everything to make things as easy as possible (aided by conventions), and to find the easiest of easy solutions. But it is clear that we have to stick with what is difficult. Everything that is alive adheres to what is difficult. Every being grows and defends itself on its own terms and assumes its unique form by relying on itself, at any cost and against all opposition. We know little, but that we have to stick with the difficult things in life is a certainty that will not leave us. It is good to be alone, for solitude is difficult. The fact that something is difficult ought to be one more reason for us to do it.

It is also good to love, for love is difficult. To love another person is perhaps the most difficult task for each of us. It is the most challenging, ultimate test and trial, the supreme work for which all other work is merely preparation. That is why young people, who are novices in everything, do not yet *know how* to love. They have to learn it. With the strengths of their entire being rallied around their lonely, timid, eagerly beating heart, they must learn to love. The time to learn something, as an apprentice, is always long and circumscribed. That is why love requires, for extended periods and into the far reaches of life: solitude, intensified and deepened solitude for the one who loves. Love, at first, does not mean anything like abandoning oneself, surrendering or becoming one with another person. (What would be a union of two unresolved, unfinished and still disorganized beings?) Love is an eminent occasion for an individual to mature and become something in and of himself, to become world, to become world for himself for the sake of another. It is a great and extravagant behest that singles him out and summons him to reach further and become more. When love is given to them, young people should use it only in this sense as the obligation to work on themselves ("to listen and to forge day and night"[1]). To abandon oneself, to give in to another person, any kind of union with others: this is not for them. They still need to conserve and prepare for a long, long time. To become oneself in love is the ultimate aim. But it may be that which today's human beings are not yet able to achieve.

Here is the serious error that young people so often

---

1 Rainer Maria Rilke, Rodin (1904).

commit. They hurl themselves at one another when love overcomes them (since it is in their nature not to have patience), and they make themselves completely available, just as they are, in all of their disorder, disarray, confusion...But what is supposed to happen next? What is life supposed to do with this pile of half smashed up things that they call their commonality and would like to call their happiness and, if that were possible, their future? Everyone loses himself for the sake of another person, but through this process loses that person and many others who wanted to come later. He loses his sense of openness, his sense of possibility, and trades in the quiet comings and goings of things that hold real promise for an infertile helplessness that can no longer yield anything. He gains nothing but a bit of disgust, disappointment and destitution, and finally escapes into one of the many social conventions that have been set up like so many storm shelters along this treacherous route. No other dimension of human experience is as generously outfitted with conventions. Various types of cleverly designed life jackets, rafts and inflatable vests: here society has succeeded in construing all kinds of escapes. Since men were inclined to treat their love life as a form of pleasure, they necessarily turned it into something flimsy, cheap, risk-free and safe, like all forms of public entertainment.

Of the many young people who love wrongly, that is by simply surrendering themselves and foregoing solitude (the average person will of course always do that), many have the uncomfortable feeling of committing an error. They want to transform the condition in which they find themselves enmeshed on their own, personal terms into something viable and fertile. For their nature tells them that all questions of love, even less so than anything else of importance, can be resolved in public and according to this or that agreement. They sense that these are genuine questions, urgent questions from one human being to another that require in each case a new, distinct, and *exclusively* personal response. But those who have already joined forces and no longer distinguish and differentiate between each other, those who no longer possess anything that is truly their own: how should they find a way out of themselves, out of the abyss where their solitude is buried?

They act out of the helplessness they have in common. When they try, in good faith, to avoid a convention that they recognize as such (for instance marriage), they get caught in the tentacles of a slightly less obvious but similarly deadly conventional solution. For everything around them now amounts to convention. *Anything* people do in the kind of murky union into which people rush early in life, is conventional. Any kind of relationship resulting from such a state of confusion is compromised, no matter how unconventional it appears on the surface (that is amoral, in everyday speech). In such a situation even a separation would be an unoriginal, conventional step and nothing but an impersonal, weak and inconclusive, arbitrary decision.

Just as for death, which is immensely difficult, for love, which is also difficult, we have not yet discovered an explanation or solution, have found no readymade answer, no marked path. There won't be a common rule reached by consensus for either one of these two tasks, which we carry deep within us and pass to others without elucidating them. But the more we live life as individuals, by drawing on our solitude, the closer we will get to these great matters. The demands that the hard work of love poses for our development are larger than life, and we cannot meet them when just starting out. But if we endure and submit to this love as a challenge and an apprenticeship, instead of losing ourselves in the facile and frivolous games which people use to hide from the most serious gravity of their existence, then those who come long after us may perhaps experience a hint of progress and relief. That would be a lot.

We are just now reaching the point where we can consider objectively and without prejudice the relationship of one human being to another. But we have no model for our attempts to live such relationships. And yet, by looking back carefully over the course of time, we glimpse a few things that can guide our timid first steps.

In their new and authentic development, girls and women will only for a brief period imitate the bad ways and the habits of men, and they will only briefly emulate male professions. Once the uncertainty of such transitions has passed, we will realize that women have adopted these (often ridiculous) disguises only in order to rid their most intimate selves of the distorting influence of the other gender. Life dwells with greater immediacy, fertility, and faith in women, and for this reason women had to evolve into more mature human beings, into more human *human* beings than man, who arrogantly and hastily fails to recognize the value of what he thinks he loves. Men only skim the surface of life; they are never pulled deeply into it by their own bodily fruit, the way women are. Once women have shed the conventions of pure femininity that they had been forced to adopt in their appearance, their true humanity, born of pain and humiliation, will emerge. And men, who still don't sense this impending change, will be surprised and defeated. One day there will be a girl, and one day there will be a woman (in the Nordic countries there are already reliable signs of this), and their names will no longer mean only the opposite of masculinity. "Girl" and "woman" each will mean something for itself that does not make one think of a lack and a limit but makes us think only of life truly lived: woman in her full humanity.

This kind of progress will transform and fundamentally change (very much against the will of men who have been surpassed) our experience of love, which currently brims with confusion. Love will no longer be a transaction between man and woman, but the relationship of one human being to another. Much closer to our humanity, this love will be infinitely considerate and quiet, and good and clear both in how it begins and how it ends. It will resemble the love that we prepare through our arduous struggles: the love of two solitudes that protect, delimit, honor, and recognize each other.

One more thing: do not believe that the great love has been lost with which you had been burdened as a boy. Didn't it produce positive and true aspirations inside of you, and a sense of purpose and resolve on which you draw to this day? I believe that this love remains so strong and powerful in your memory because it was your first deep experience of being alone, and because it became the first inner work you applied to your life.

Those who are loved live badly and dangerously. Alas, if only they would outlast themselves and become lovers. Lovers are surrounded by nothing but safety.

Is IT not wonderful, first of all, to assure oneself that love can lead to such strength, and that at bottom it concerns something that exceeds us entirely, and that nonetheless the heart is bold enough to embark on this going-beyond-us, this tempest for which an entire genesis would be required?

IF YOU tried only this: to be the hand in my hand

as in the wineglass is the wine.

If you tried only this.

To TAKE love seriously, to endure it, and to learn it the way one learns a profession—that is what young people need to do. People have misunderstood the role of love in life like so many other things. They have turned love into a game and something fun because they thought that games and fun are more blissful than work; but nothing is filled with greater joy and happiness than work, and love, exactly because it is the most extreme joy and happiness, can be nothing but work.—Someone in love thus has to try to behave as if he had to accomplish a major task: he has to spend a lot of time alone, reflect, collect himself and hold on to himself; he has to work; he has to become something!

A BELOVED who gives in is still far from being a lover.

THERE is no force in the world but love, and when you carry it within you, when you simply *have* it, even if you remain baffled as to *how* to use it, it will work its radiant effects and help you out of and beyond yourself: one must never lose this faith, one must simply— (and if it were nothing else) endure in it!

In the kind of love that is called "sensual" with an insufferable mix of disdain, desire and curiosity, one finds the worst effects of that denigration which Christianity thinks it must inflict on our earthly existence. Here everything is distortion and repression, even though we are the products of this deepest experience, which we claim as our own in the center of our raptures. It is increasingly incomprehensible to me how a discipline that blames us for being wrong in the area where we enjoy our most blissful right as complete beings, can continue to impose itself on us, even if it nowhere proves worthy.

You alone make me. Only you I can exchange.

For a bit it's you, then again the rumbling waves,

or a scent without a trace.

Ah, I lost them all in my embrace,

only you are always born again:

because I never held onto you, I hold you tight.

To BE a part, that is fulfillment for us: to be integrated with our solitude into a state that can be shared.

IT IS only a step from the devotion of a lover to the devotion of the lyric poet.

ARE not all true relations outside of convention?

WE have, when we love, nothing but this: to let each other be, for holding on to each other is easy and nothing we yet need to learn.

FROM one human being to another everything is so difficult, unrehearsed and without a model and example that one would have to live within every relationship with absolute attention and be creative in every moment that requires something new and poses tasks, questions and demands.

IF YOU discover that you frighten yourself upon recognizing that you become uncontrolled, terrifying and even a torment for the other person whom you have conquered in love, then you might wish to conjure a mental counterimage showing that the conquest and ownership of another human being—so that one could use this person for one's own (often so fatefully conditioned) pleasure;—that the use of another human being does not exist, must not exist, cannot exist—and you will regain the distance and awe that will compel you to adjust your excitement according to standards established during your courtship. It happens frequently that the kind of happiness, such as that experienced by you in loving and being loved, unleashes not only new forces in a young man but uncovers entirely different, deeper layers of his nature from which then the most uncanny findings erupt overwhelmingly: but our confusions have always been part of our riches, and where their violence scares us we are simply startled by the unfathomed possibilities and tensions of our strength—and this chaos, as soon as we gain some distance from it, immediately triggers within us the premonition of new orders and, if we can enlist our courage in such premonitions even just a bit, the curiosity and desire to achieve this unforeseeable future order! I have written "distance;" should there be anything like advice that I would be able to suggest to you, it would be the hunch that you need to search for *that* now, for distance. Distance: from the current consternation and from those new conditions and proliferations of your soul that you enjoyed when they first happened but which you have not yet truly claimed as your own. A short isolation and separation of a few weeks, a period of reflection, and a new focusing of your crowded and unbridled nature would offer the greatest probability of rescuing all of that which right now seems to be destroying itself in and through your persistence.

Nothing locks people in error as much as the daily repetition of error—and how many individuals who ended up bound to each other in a frozen fate could have secured for themselves, by means of a few small, pure separations, that rhythm through which their hearts' mysterious mobility would have inexhaustibly persisted in the depth of their inner world-space, through every alteration and change.

THIS is one of the most unconditional tasks of friendship: to be pure in every No, wherever one is not absolutely flooded with the most infinite Yes.

When love ends...

You, already lost from the start,

beloved, who never arrived,

I don't know what sounds you adore.

I no longer try, when the future swells up,

to recognize you. All the immense

images in me: landscapes experienced at a
distance,

cities and towers and bridges and un-

expected turns in our paths,

and the powerful countries once

suffused with the Gods,

rise up within me to mean

you, who eludes me.

You are the gardens, alas,

I gazed at with such unbridled

hope. A window left open

in a country house—and you almost

stepped, pensively, toward me. I discovered alleys,—

you had just walked them,

and sometimes the mirrors in stores

were still dizzy with you and returned, startled,

my too sudden image.—Who knows, whether the same

bird did not call through both of us,

separately, last night?

WHY do people in love break up before it becomes necessary to do so?—Indeed, perhaps because this necessity may come up and impose itself at any moment. Because it is something yet so very provisional: to be together and to be in love. Because behind it there lurks in everyone the peculiar certainty—often admitted, often denied—that everything that surpasses our pleasant and inherently non-progressive state of equilibrium will have to be received, tolerated, and mastered by an infinitely solitary (nearly singular) individual who is completely alone. The hour of dying, which extracts this insight from everyone, is only one of our hours and not an exception. Our being continually passes through and into transformations that might be no less intense than the new, near, and next states ushered in by death. And just as we must leave each other irrevocably at a specific moment in this most conspicuous of changes, we must, strictly speaking, give up and let the other move on without tying them down at every moment. Does it disturb you that I can write all this down, like someone copying a sentence in a foreign language who does not realize that it expresses the greatest pain? I can do so because this terrible truth is probably at the same time our most productive and blissful truth. Although it loses none of its severe sublimity even when we contemplate it frequently (and even if one were to curl up around it tearfully, one would neither warm nor mollify it), our faith in its strength and difficulty grows every day. And suddenly one can imagine, as if through clear tears, the distant realization that even as a lover one needs to be alone. This insight might be painful but not unjust, even when it seizes and shuts us in just as our feelings surge toward the beloved. It is the realization that even this apparently most shared of experiences, which is love, can be fully developed and, in a way, perfected only when one is alone and apart from others. For the joining of strong tendencies results in a current of pleasure that sweeps us along and finally casts us out somewhere else, while an individual enclosed in his feelings will experience love as a daily task to be performed on himself, and as the incessant creation of bold and magnanimous challenges imposed on the other. People who are thus in love with each other summon infinite dangers around them, but they are safe from the petty perils that have worn out and eroded so many great beginnings of true emotion. Since they continually wish for and challenge each other to achieve something extreme, neither of them can treat the other unjustly by imposing a limit; on the contrary, they incessantly create for one another more space and room and freedom, just as someone who loves God has always flung from his heart and instituted God's plenitude and absolute power in the depths of the heavens. That illustrious beloved has had the cautious wisdom and (it cannot be misunderstood when phrased this way) even used the noble ruse of never revealing himself. Thus for a few ecstatic souls, the love of God could lead to imaginary moments of pleasure—and yet, according to its essence, it has always remained work through and through, a most demanding chore and a most difficult effort.

ULTIMATELY nobody can help anyone else in life; one has this recurring experience in every conflict and confusion: that one is alone. This is not as bad as it may appear at first glance; it is also the best thing about life that everyone contains everything within himself: his fate, his future, his entire scope and world. Now there surely exist moments when it is difficult to be within oneself and to endure within oneself. It happens that precisely when one ought to hold on to oneself more tightly and—one would almost have to say—more obstinately than ever, one attaches oneself to something external, and that during important events one shifts one's proper center out of oneself to something strange, into another human being. This is against the most basic principles of equilibrium and can lead to nothing but great difficulty.

READ Plato's *Symposium:* "Eros is not beautiful," if Eros were beautiful and charitable, there ought to be no complaints, but Eros is hard, needy, distress for the sake of another, an appeal to this other, such a vast, blessed, stormy demand of this other to be beautiful, powerful and loving—that he would have to turn into a God with all of his blood not to be left behind.

A Woman in Love

This is my window. I just
so gently awoke. I thought
I was floating. How far
extends my life, and where
begins the night?

I could have thought that all
around me was still nothing but I,
clear like a crystal's
depth, darkened and mute.

I still could grasp the stars
in me, so vast
my heart seems now, so much
I would like to let him go,

the one I perhaps began to love,

perhaps began to hold.

Strange, like never yet described,

my fate looks back at me.
How I am placed

beneath this infinity,

fragrant like a meadow

that is moved to-and-fro,

while calling out with dread

so that another hears the call

whose devastation it becomes

in someone else's soul.

IT IS a disturbing thought that the instant of love that we experience so fully, profoundly, and peculiarly as our own could be so entirely determined beyond the individual person by the future (the future child) and, on the other side, by the past. But even *then:* this moment of love would retain its indescribable depth as an escape into oneself. Which I strongly tend to believe. This would correspond to our experience of how the incommensurate moments of our most profound rapture occur as if they had been lifted out of time itself. Such experiences truly run perpendicular to the directions of life, just as death runs perpendicular in relation to them, and they have more in common with death than with all of the aims and movements of our vitality. Only death (when it is not regarded as a state of withered decay but presumed to be the intensity that quite exceeds us) affords us a perspective to do justice to love. But here our vision is obstructed and distorted in all directions by the common understanding of these quantities. Our traditions have lost their power to transmit; have become spindly branches no longer nourished from the power of the root. And once we add to this the absentmindedness, distractedness, and impatience of man, and the fact that woman is profoundly giving only in the rare relationships of happiness, and that next to these thus splintered and shaken individuals the child stands as something which already surpasses them while remaining just as helpless—well, then one might humbly admit that things are quite difficult for us.

It is a miracle that man has lasted this long, since he has been involved in love always only in his most threadbare spots. What a pathetic figure man cuts in the history of love. He has almost no strength besides the superiority that tradition ascribes to him, and even this superiority he bears so carelessly that it would be outrageous if this distractedness and absent-heartedness were not sometimes partly justified by important events. Yet nobody will talk me out of what is plain to see between this most extreme lover [the 17th-century Portuguese nun Marianna Alcoforado] and her shameful partner: that this relation definitively proves how everything that has been achieved, endured, and accomplished in love exists on the part of women, while on the part of men, there is absolute inadequacy in love. She is practically awarded, to use a banal analogy, the diploma in the art of love, while he carries an elementary grammar book in this discipline in his pocket, from which, at best, he has picked up a few words to construct an occasional sentence, as pretty and thrilling as the well-known sentences on the first pages of a language primer.

PEOPLE are so terribly far apart from each other, and people in love are often at the furthest distance. They throw all that is their own to the other person who fails to catch it, and it ends up in a pile somewhere between them and finally prevents them from seeing and walking toward each other.

WHY did they make our sex homeless, instead of assigning the festival of our responsibility to it?...Why do we have to slink around it, and finally gain access to it like criminals and thieves?—Why are guilt and sin not attached to another part of our body?

WORLD had been in the beloved's face—,

but suddenly poured out:

World is outside, world cannot be seized.

Why didn't I drink, when I lifted it up,

from the full, beloved countenance,

world, so close, beautifully scented, near my mouth?

Alas, I drank. How tirelessly I drank.

But I was also filled up with too much

world, and, drinking, passed beyond it, too.

THIS is what guilt means, if there is guilt at all: not to grant more freedom to a lover.

I THINK that a person who has lost love never acquired love.

ALL disagreements and misunderstandings originate in the fact that people search for commonality *within* themselves instead of searching for it in the things *behind* them, in the light, in the landscape, in beginning, and in death. By so doing they lose themselves and gain nothing in turn.

As SOON as two people have resolved to give up on being together, the resulting pain, with its heaviness or particularity, is already so completely part of the life of each individual that the other has to firmly stop himself from becoming sentimental and from feeling pity. The beginning of the agreed-upon separation is marked precisely by this pain, and its first challenge will be that this *pain* belongs *already* separately to each of the two individuals. This pain is an essential condition for what the now solitary and loneliest individual will have to create, in the future, from his reclaimed life.

If TWO people managed not to get mired in hatred during their honest struggles with each other, that is, caught on the edges of their passion that became ragged and sharp when it cooled and set, if they could stay fluid, active, flexible, and changeable in all of their interactions and relations, and, in a word, if a mutually human and friendly consideration remained available to them, then their decision to separate cannot easily conjure disaster and terror.

WHEN a separation is concerned, pain should already belong in its entirety to that other life from which you wish to separate. Otherwise the two individuals will continually grow soft toward each other and cause helpless and unproductive suffering. During the process of a firmly agreed-upon separation, however, the pain itself constitutes an important investment in the renewal and fresh start that both sides want to reach. People in your situation might have to communicate as friends. But for a certain time, these two separated lives should remain *without* any knowledge of each other and exist as far apart and as detached from the other as possible. This is necessary so that each life can base itself firmly on its new needs and circumstances. Any subsequent contact (which may then be truly new and perhaps very happy) has to be left to unpredictable patterns and directions.

DEPARTURES create a burden within our emotions. The distance stays behind them with greater emphasis and works and grows and gains hold of all the commonalities that ought to remain instinctive even for those who are very far apart...

LOOK at the lovers,

when hardly they have started confessing,

how soon they lie.

CLARA [Rilke's wife] and I, dear Friedrich [Rilke's son-in-law], found ourselves and understood each other exactly in the realization that true togetherness can last when two solitudes are allowed to grow next to each other, and that everything that is commonly called devotion is in its essence detrimental to being-together. For when a person takes leave of himself, he is nothing any longer, and when two people abandon themselves in order to encounter each another, there is no more ground beneath them and their being-together is a continual falling.—We have, my dear Friedrich, experienced this not without great pain, and have thus experienced what anyone wishing for his own life will learn either way.

THERE is only one deadly mistake we can make: to attach ourselves to another human being, even if only for an instant.

FOR love is the actual climate of fate: no matter how far its path extends through the heavens, its milky way composed of millions of stars of blood, the land beneath those heavens lies pregnant with disaster. Not even the Gods, in the transformation of their passion, were sufficiently powerful to liberate the startled, earthly beloved from the entanglements of this fertile soil.

THERE is no more wretched prison than the fear of hurting a person who loves you.

To BECOME superfluous somewhere means to need only yourself: if you are asked to end something, this also means that you are receiving an order to begin anew; a new beginning is always possible—who should refuse it?

When love endures...

To BE loved means to flare up. To love is: to glow with inexhaustible oil. To be loved is to vanish; to love is to last.

Look, we do not love, like flowers, complete

in a single year; when we love,

primordial sap wells up in our limbs.

Is LOVE, together with art, not the only license to surpass the human condition and to be greater, more generous, more unhappy, if necessary, than common man? Let us be this way, heroically, and let us not reject any of the advantages that this state of agitation bestows on us.

THIS is the miracle that occurs each time with those who truly love: the more they give, the more they possess the kind of delicious, nourishing love that gives flowers and children their strength, and that could help everyone if people would only accept it without doubt or hesitation.

WITH just a bit of innocence and pleasure taken in reality (which is entirely independent of time), it would never have occurred to people to think that they could ever again lose something to which they had truly attached themselves. No constellation of stars is as steadfast, no achievement as irrevocable as relations among human beings that, starting at the moment when they are first visibly formed, take root with far greater force in the realm of the invisible: in those depths where our existence is as permanent as gold lodged in rock, more lasting than a star.

Two individuals who are quiet to the same degree have no need to talk about the melody of their hours. This melody is what they have in common in and of themselves. Like a burning altar, it hovers between them, and they feed the sacred flame respectfully with an occasional word. If I were to lift these two individuals out of their unintentional existence and place them on an imaginary stage, it would clearly be my intent to show two lovers, and to explain why they feel so blessed. On the stage, however, the altar is invisible and nobody knows how to interpret the strange gestures made by these individuals in the ritual sacrifice.

ALL of love is an effort for me, an achievement, *work past my limits;* only with regard to God are matters a bit easier, because to love God means to enter, walk, stand, rest, and be everywhere in God's love.

WOMAN has undergone, suffered, and achieved what is most proper to her all the way to its completion. Man, who could always use the excuse of being occupied with more important matters and (let's be frank) who also was not sufficiently prepared for love, has since antiquity not permitted himself (with the exception of the saints) to engage with love. The troubadours knew exactly how little they were permitted to advance, and Dante, for whom this became an extremely pressing need, could only get around love on the awesome ellipsis of his gigantically evasive poem. Everything else, in this sense, is derivative and secondary.

To LOVE means to be alone.

THERE is no general response to your husband's question that you pose to me in your letter. Only the most *personal* solution in each particular case will make it clear whether or not a person causes damage to himself by sacrificing something for another. Even when someone seems to renounce his own ideals out of solicitude for another person, this does not have to lead to complete renunciation but can become an opportunity. A person who makes a strong effort on behalf of someone else, in a great gesture of subjugation, might yet again harness within the other person *that* which he neglects in himself. And some people might consider it more beautiful and rewarding to blossom in a beloved person or in a greatly conceived community, rather than in their own being.

To PUT it like this: it is indeed us, once we seize the tentative happiness of love with our hands, who may be the first to destroy it. It should remain on the anvil of its creator, subjected to the blows of his hardworking hammer. Let us place our confidence in this admirable craftsman: it is true that we always feel the poundings of his tool, which he wields mercilessly according to the rules of a perfected art. But to counteract this, we are also from time to time called upon to admire his favorite work as he guides it toward ultimate perfection: how much we had already admired it this first time! We are involved in our love as collaborators to an extremely small degree; this is exactly why our love is immune to trivial dangers. Let it become our task to get to know its laws, its seasons, its rhythms, and the progression of its constellations across its vast, starry sky. Take a moment to consider this, my friend, and consider it well!! I know well that in speaking to you in this fashion, there remains an absolutely unequal task for the two of us: you are too much woman not to suffer infinitely, *because of the deferral of love that seems to be required by this task.* And, as far as I am concerned, by gathering completely around my work, I secure the means of my most definitive happiness, while you, at least at this moment, in turning toward your life find yourself encumbered by semi-petrified tasks. Don't be discouraged by this; it will surely change. The transfiguration of your heart will gradually allow you to influence the remaining obstacles of reality; everything that seems impenetrable to you will be rendered transparent by your blazing heart...Don't think too much about the moment and guard against judging life in those hazy hours that afford us no glimpse of its vastness.

I AM of the opinion that "marriage" as such does not deserve as much emphasis as it receives due to the conventional development of its nature. Nobody dreams of demanding that an unattached individual should be "happy"—once someone is married, however, everyone is very astonished when he is *not!* (Meanwhile, it actually isn't all that important to be happy, neither as a single nor as a married person.) In some regards, marriage simplifies the conditions of life, and such a union surely augments the strengths and determinations of two young people so that together they seem to reach further into the future than before.—Except, all of these are sensations on which one cannot live. Marriage is, above all, a new task and a new seriousness—a new challenge and a question regarding the strength and kindness of each participant, and a new great danger for both.

In marriage, in my opinion, the point is not to achieve a rapid union by tearing down and toppling all boundaries. Rather, the good marriage is the kind where each person appoints the other as guardian of his solitude, and thus demonstrates to the other person the greatest faith he can bestow. The *being-together* of two human beings is an impossibility and, where it nonetheless seems to be present, it is a limitation, a mutual agreement that robs one or both parties of their fullest freedom and development. Yet once it is recognized that even among the *closest* individuals there extend infinite distances, a wonderful coexistence can develop when they succeed in loving the vastness between them, which affords them the possibility of seeing each other as complete figures before a great sky!

This, therefore, has to be the measure for one's rejection or acceptance of marriage: whether one wants to stand guard over another person's solitude, and whether one is inclined to position this same person at the gates of one's own depth, of whose existence he will learn only through what issues forth from a great darkness, clad in festive garb.

MARRIAGE is difficult, and those who take it seriously are beginners who suffer and learn!

I ALSO stand silently and full of deep trust *before* the gates of this solitude, because I consider this to be the highest task in the union of two people: that one stands guard over the other's solitude. If the essence of both indifference and the crowd consists in not acknowledging solitude, then love and friendship exist to continually furnish opportunities for solitude. And only these commonalities are genuine that rhythmically interrupt deep states of loneliness...Remember the time when you first got to know Clara Westhoff [Rilke's wife]: then your love waited patiently for a gate to open, the same love that now impatiently taps at the walls behind which things are happening that we do not know, that I know as little as you—only that I have faith that they will touch me deeply and intimately, once they reveal themselves to me. Can your love not find a similar faith? Based on this faith alone, you will experience joys that will sustain your love without going hungry.

In such a case [of a fight with a loved one] it is time (in my personal opinion) to withdraw into oneself and to approach neither one nor the other person and to resist referring the suffering they now experience back to the cause of suffering (which lies so far outside), but to make it productive for yourself. If you move what is happening with your feeling into solitude and keep your wavering and trembling sensations out of the dangerous proximity of magnetic forces, then it will assume on its own and with its innate agility the position that is natural and inevitable for it.—It helps, in any case, to remind yourself very frequently that everything in existence is governed by laws that never stop working but rather rush to prove and test themselves on every stone and every feather dropped by us. Whenever we are in error, then, such erring is nothing but the failure to recognize by which laws we are governed in a specific case. Any possible solution will begin with our attention and concentration, which quietly integrates us into the chain of events and restores to our will its swaying counterweights.

IT IS in the nature of every absolute love that sooner or later it reaches the beloved only in infinity.

But so deeply is death rooted in the essence of love (if we only let ourselves know death, without allowing ourselves to be distracted by the ugliness and suspicions people attribute to it), that it nowhere contradicts love. Into *what* place, finally, can death drive the one thing that we had sheltered in our heart with such wordless intensity, if not *into* this very heart? Where would be the "idea" of the beloved person and his unceasing influence (for *how* could *this* influence have ceased since already during their lifetime it had begun to work independently of his or her tangible presence)? Where would this effect, which is always already hidden from us, be more secure than *within* us?! Where can we get closer to it, celebrate it more purely, submit to it better than there where it occurs in harmony with our own voices, as if our heart had mastered a new language, a new song, a new strength!

LOVE does not care about our divisions but pulls us, trembling as we are, into an infinite awareness of the whole.

WE may have suspected it, though it may never have been shown to us as clearly, that the essence of love does not consist in togetherness but in the way one individual compels the other to become something, become infinitely great, become the most for which his powers may suffice.

To LOVE is difficult. And when someone calls on you to love, he gives you a great task, but not an impossible one. He does not call on you to love another human being, which is nothing for beginners, and he does not demand for you to love a God, which only the most mature can accomplish. He only draws your attention to what is difficult for you, which is your most humble and most fertile spot at once.

IT IS horrible that we have no religion where these experiences, namely acts of love, as literal and tangible as they are (at the same time so ineffable and so inviolable), can be elevated into God, into the protection of a phallic deity that might have to be the *first* with which a whole group of Gods will intrude again upon mankind, after such a long absence. What else could be of assistance when religion fails to help us—by suppressing these experiences instead of transfiguring them, and by depriving us of them instead of implanting them in us more magnificently than we might dare imagine. Here we have been infinitely abandoned and betrayed: this causes the disaster we find ourselves in. When the religions became systems of moral philosophy by burning out on the surfaces and adding ever more burnt-out surfaces, they displaced this experience, the innermost of their and our existence, to the cold ground of morality and thus, necessarily, to the periphery. We will gradually realize that the great catastrophe of our time occurs *here,* and not in the social or economic domain—in this repression of the act of love to the periphery. All the strengths of insightful individuals are now wasted by shifting the act of love back at least into their *own* center (since it is already not in the general center of the world, which would prompt the world to be instantly reordered by new Gods!).—Those who move through life blindly, on the contrary, somehow enjoy the accessibility of "pleasure" now located on the periphery and take revenge for their worthlessness there. In an act that is unwittingly clear-minded, they seek out this pleasure that they nonetheless despise.—Superficial renunciation does *not* constitute progress, and it makes no sense to summon one's "willpower" for this purpose (which is in any case too recent a force in comparison with the ancient righteousness of our drives). Renunciation of love and fulfillment of love: both are wonderful and without equal only in the place where the experience of love as a whole can assume a central position, with *all* of its nearly indistinguishable thrills (which alternate in such a way that *there* the psychic and the physical can no longer be distinguished): that is then also the place (in the ecstasy of a few lovers and saints of *all* times and *all* religions) where renunciation and fulfillment become identical. Where infinity occurs *entirely* (whether as a negative or positive), the prefix drops away, that which had been the, alas, all too humanly achieved way, which now has been followed—and what remains is the state of having arrived, the state of *being* itself!

IT IS a characteristic of every deepened love that it makes us just and clairvoyant.

There are two events in our lives, according to poet Rainer Maria Rilke, that let us experience something greater than human existence: death, which tears us out of life in ways we still do not understand, and love, which does so in ways both wonderful and overwhelming. Love was a powerful and transformative event for Rilke, who composed a series of love poems in addition to the cycles of poems about everyday things that disclose the beauty and terror of the world, among them his famous *Sonnets to Orpheus* (1922) and the *Duino Elegies* (1912-22). We can become *more* in love than what and who we usually are. In the best of cases, which can be a love that lasts a week or one that lasts a lifetime, we grow alongside, for, and with the person we love.

Rilke cared deeply about all of the dimensions of love: falling in love, being in love, fighting for love, fighting against love, being loved, and living beyond love. He fell in love several times in his life—with the writer Lou Andreas-Salomé (his muse and mentor who was nearly fifteen years his senior), for the painter Paula Modersohn-Becker (whose untimely death at age thirty-one prompted him to write the 1908 elegy "Requiem: For a Friend," and several other artists, musicians, and writers. The most resonant passages from among the fifteen thousand letters he wrote (before his untimely death in 1926, at age fifty-one), together with the most incisive and deepest reflections on love from his poetry, are gathered in this book. They have been translated for this volume anew to capture the vitality and precision that makes Rilke's writing so impactful for readers in many languages. Rilke's resonance with so many poets everywhere has produced fine and often inspired translations into English and other languages, many by poets and writers whose names are familiar to American readers: Stephen Mitchell, Edward A. Snow, Galway Kinnell, Ruth Speirs, Damion Searls, Alfred Poulin, Michael Hamburger, William H. Gass, John J. L. Mood, Mary D. Herter Norton, Allan Corns, Anita Barrows, Joanna Macy, and many more. Each translator has produced his or her version of Rilke's words, often with startlingly moving results. I have greatly benefited from all of them. I have read them as much as feats of interpretation as renderings of Rilke, since I hear the poet with the ear of someone whose native tongue is German and who acquired English (after French) as a third, yet ever-widening path, through my being—to borrow a phrase from the *Duino Elegies*—"not very reliably at home / in the interpreted world."

Rilke believed that living and loving—consciously, attentively, and with real intention—teach us everything. He also believed that we are usually too distracted by the things we consider important to recognize and learn from the lessons life teaches us, and that we often confuse our own instincts, or consider them pure and unambiguous, when in fact they are anything but that. His writings do not lay out a program on *how* to live, but offer advice—for situations ranging from the first excitement of young love, to sexuality, marriage, and spiritual love. Rilke reminds us, in powerful and precise words, that all we need to know is already given to us, if only we are open to the great risks and the great rewards harbored by love.

Rainer Maria Rilke

René Karl Wilhelm Johann Josef Maria Rilke was born on December 4, 1875, in Prague, then part of the Austro-Hungarian Empire, to railroad inspector Joseph and Sophie (Phia) Rilke (born Entz), part of the minority German-speaking community of Prague.

By the time Rilke was ten, his parents had separated. They enrolled him at a military boarding school in St. Pölten, Austria, when he was eleven years old, with the expectation that he should become an officer—an ambition that he did not share. He transferred to a German preparatory school, and, although a gifted student, he dropped out before graduating. He then entered a trade school in Linz, Austria, while preparing privately for the entrance exams for Charles-Ferdinand University in Prague. By the time he enrolled there in 1895, Rilke had already published his first collection of poems, *Lives and Songs* (1894). After a year of studying art history, philosophy, and literature in Prague, he transferred to a university in Munich where he mingled in literary circles, published two poetry collections, short stories, and plays, and was introduced to the work of Danish writer Jens Peter Jacobsen, who exercised a powerful influence on Rilke during his formative years.

On a trip to Venice in 1897, Rilke met Lou Andreas-Salomé, a married woman fifteen years his senior who became his lover, mentor, and muse and famously instructed him to shorten his given names to the more masculine Rainer and impose more discipline on his prodigious poetic talents. Their romantic relationship lasted four years, and their friendship a lifetime. After spending the summer of 1897 with Salomé and her husband in the Bavarian Alps, Rilke accompanied them to Berlin and settled there. In 1898 he published a collection of prose sketches, *Am Leben hin (Near Life)*. Over the next several years Rilke traveled widely: first to Italy with Salomé and her husband, followed by two significant trips with Salomé to Russia, where he met with writers Leonid Pasternak and Leo Tolstoy. Rilke visited an artists' colony in Worpswede (in northern Germany) at the invitation of painter Heinrich Vogeler in 1900, where he met the painter Paula Modersohn-Becker and the sculptor Clara Westhoff, who had been a pupil of the French sculptor Auguste Rodin. The following year he married Clara Westhoff and the Rilkes' only child, daughter Ruth, was born. The Rilkes separated soon after their daughter's birth but remained in contact for the rest of Rilke's life.

In 1902, Rilke befriended Rodin and published *The Book of Images*, his first full book of poetry, and the commissioned monograph *Auguste Rodin*. Rilke was based in Paris for the next twelve years, during which time he traveled to Italy, Germany, Sweden, Spain, Algiers, Tunis, Egypt, and many other locations. He published his first great work, *The Book of Hours*, in 1905, followed by *New Poems* (1907), *The New Poems: Second Part* (1908), and his only novel about a young Danish man living in the modern metropolis of Paris, *The Notebooks of Malte Laurids Brigge* (1910). During these formative years, Rilke experienced several upheavals. His father died in 1906 and he and Rodin, whose personal assistant he had been, had a falling out after the poet contacted one of Rodin's clients. (They eventually reconciled.) Rilke met and fell in love with Mimi Romanelli, the youngest sister of the Italian art dealer Pietro Romanelli known for her beauty and musical talent. Rilke stayed in her family's small hotel in Venice in 1907. After a brief romantic relationship they maintained a long correspondence.

Rilke spent part of the winter of 1911 at Duino Castle (owned by the aristocratic family Thurn and Taxis) in Northern Italy, near Trieste, where he began the first of the Duino *Elegies*. Rilke was in Munich at the outbreak of World War 1, and as a foreign national he was not permitted to return to Paris. Despite attempts to defer enlistment, he was conscripted into the Austro-Hungarian army and called to active duty in 1916, which he served largely in administrative roles. After six months, his friends interceded and he was discharged. With the end of the war and the dissolution of the Austro-Hungarian empire, Rilke was stateless for a period before becoming a citizen of the newly established Czech Republic. The period from 1912 to 1920 is often regarded as a creative crisis for Rilke, even though he wrote hundreds of poems published only posthumously, and a great number of letters to friends, former lovers, patrons and anyone whose letters had moved him, and that he considered, in a formal last will, to be as important as his poetic works.

After settling in Munich, Rilke had a brief relationship with the writer Claire Studer (later the wife of poet Yvan Goll). The two remained friends until Rilke's death. In 1919, Rilke began a relationship with the painter Baladine Klossowska, in whose two sons, Pierre (who became a writer and philosopher), and Balthasar (the painter Balthus) he took a great interest. Rilke wrote the text for a small book of cat paintings by Balthus that was published when the painter was twelve years of age.

After several attempts to gain a residency permit for Switzerland, Rilke finally moved into a modest stone house, called Château de Muzot, near Sierre in the Swiss canton Valais, which was initially leased and then purchased for him by a wealthy sponsor, Werner Reinhart. There, in the span of about a week, he completed the *Duino Elegies* and wrote the *Sonnets to Orpheus.* Rilke considered both works, which appeared in 1923, the culmination of his creative output.

For the next three years Rilke's poor health forced him to spend extended periods in a sanatorium in Val-Mont sur Territet near Lake Geneva. He was intermittently able to receive guests, including Paul Valéry and Clara Westhoff, who visited him in 1924. He spent much of the following year in Paris, returning to Muzot in August. As his health continued to deteriorate, Rilke was in and out of Val-Mar. Rilke died of leukemia on December 29, 1926, and was buried on January 2, 1927, at the cemetery in Raron. A posthumous publication of his poetry in six volumes, *Collected Works,* appeared in the fall; his widow, daughter and son-in-law became literary executors who published the first series of letters and some of the uncollected poems.

Rilke's reputation has grown steadily since his death, and he has come to be universally regarded as one of the most original poets in the literary canon.

Contemplations
Great Minds on What Matters

DICKINSON on Love
NIETZSCHE on Love
RILKE on Love
WILDE ON LOVE
PROUST on Love
SHAKESPEARE on Love
THE GREEKS on Love
THE ROMANTICS on Love

Current and forthcoming titles in the
Warbler Press Contemplations series at
warblerpress.com

9 781734 588125